EQUALITY

&

DIVERSITY

IN THE WORK PLACE

AN OVERVIEW OF THE PRINCIPLES AND LAW GOVERNING EQUALITY AND DIVERSITY

I0402285

JOSHUA   JOGO

Copyright © 2015 Joshua Jogo

Disclaimer

All the material contained in this book is provided for educational and informational purposes only. No responsibility can be taken for any results or outcomes resulting from the use of this material. While every attempt has been made to provide information that is both accurate and effective, the author does not assume any responsibility for the accuracy or use/misuse of this information.

PUBLISHED IN THE UNITED KINGDOM BY GLOBAL HEATHROW GATEWAY PUBLISHING UK, HEATHROW HOUSE, LONDON.

Tel: UK: +447448522120
Tel: US: +19293235293
Email: joshuajogo@hotmail.com
Web: **www.joshuajogo.com**
Publishing rights administered on Amazon by HGPUK

Presented To:

_____

From:

_____

Date:

_____

Sign:

_____

INTRODUCTION

This book introduces you to the basic principles of Equality & Diversity.

Take as many notes as you need during READING - sometimes it's a good way of retaining some important information that you might need when it comes to the knowledge check.

The main Objectives are to have knowledge of the protected characteristics as defined in the Equality Act 2010.

Explain the different types of discrimination that exist and could impact you and/or your colleagues

Describe the key equality issues you should be mindful of from recruitment through to promotion, up to and including retirement.

Provide good practice advice relating to the key equality issues

Describe your responsibilities under the Modern Slavery Act and what to do if you suspect there's an issue.

Explain the important ways in which we can promote equality & diversity in the workplace.

Ask the question 'What is Equality and Diversity' and you will hear many answers. There is much confusion, it is often obscured by myths and most people are wary of dealing with Equality and Diversity issues for fear that they may do or say something wrong. Our Equality and Diversity module aims to dispel these myths.

CONTENTS

Chapter 1: - What is Equality & Diversity?
This chapter looks at the difference between Equality & Diversity and introduces you to the Equality Act 2010

Chapter 2: - Discrimination
Here you will learn about the different types of discrimination and see some working examples. You'll also be introduced to the 9 Protected Characteristics in the Equality Act

Chapter 3: - Key Equality Issues
Learn more about some of the key equality issues you may be faced with in the workplace with some best practice ideas that will help

Chapter 4: - Diverse People, Diverse Identities
How do we manage Diversity at City? Why do we make assumptions and what are the consequences of doing so? Learn more in this chapter

Chapter 5: - Modern Slavery

Modern Slavery is on the increase with an estimated 13,000 victims in the UK. This chapter helps you to recognise some of the potential signs of slavery and what to do if you become suspicious

CHAPTER ONE

Equality & Diversity Knowledge Check
Put all of your knowledge to the test with this multiple choice knowledge check

What is Equality & Diversity?

Equality and Diversity don't mean the same thing, but they are closely related.

We need to make sure that we note and value these differences (diversity) if we're going to make sure everyone has equal rights and opportunities (equality)

What is Equality & Diversity?
Equality can mean many different things to many different people but essentially it's about making sure that everyone is treated fairly.

It can be described as:

Removing barriers people may face due to actual or perceived differences.
Eliminating discrimination
Making sure that everyone has the same access to opportunities

If you've read the definition for **Diversity** click on the next arrow below to find out why they are important.
Equality and Diversity don't mean the same thing, but they are closely related.

We need to make sure that we note and value these differences (diversity) if we're going to make sure everyone has equal rights and opportunities (equality).

What is Equality & Diversity?

Diversity is about recognizing, valuing and considering people's different backgrounds, knowledge, skills and experiences.

It's also about helping to create a productive and effective workforce.

If you've read the definition for **Equality** click on the next arrow below to find out why they are important.

Equality and Diversity don't mean the same thing, but they are closely related.

We need to make sure that we note and value these differences (diversity) if we're going to make sure everyone has equal rights and opportunities (equality)

What is the law?
The Equality Act 2010 is a law which protects you from discrimination.

It aims to prevent people from being treated differently or unfairly on the basis of specific characteristics.

The act replaced most of the previous anti-discrimination laws with a single act to make the law much simpler and easy for people to understand and comply with.

The act aims to reduce unfair treatment in the workplace (and in wider society) particularly when employers are dealing with areas such as recruitment, training, promotion and equal pay.

CHAPTER TWO

Discrimination

Discrimination is the unfair treatment of an individual or group of individuals based on an actual or perceived characteristics (linked to the Equality Act list of protected characteristic)

The Act defines four main types of discrimination:

Direct discrimination
Indirect discrimination
Harassment
Victimisation

Before we explore each one in more detail watch a short 5 minute video that will introduce each type and introduce you to the 9 protected characteristics mentioned on the previous page.

Test your knowledge so far:

Before we move, let's test what you've learned so far.

Click on the correct answer then click on **Submit my answer** for instant feedback

Question:

One of your colleagues, Gary, is an atheist and does not have any religious beliefs. You hear another one of your colleagues, Walter, constantly taunting him about this. Which one of the characteristics might Gary be protected under?

Race

Religion and Belief

None of the above

Introduction

Tinu from ACAS has just described how direct discrimination occurs when one individual is treated less favourably than another individual.

Let's take some time now to look at it in a bit more detail and think more about how it can affect us in the workplace.

What's direct discrimination?

Direct discrimination occurs when someone is treated less favourably than another person because of a protected characteristic they have or are thought to have (see discrimination by perception), or because they associate with someone who has a protected characteristic (see discrimination by association)

What's discrimination by association?

This is direct discrimination against someone because they associate with another person who possesses a protected characteristic.

Imagine, Ailsa becoming the subject of discriminatory remarks and being hassled because she goes to lunch every day with Max, who is a Rastafarian.

What's discrimination by perception?

This is direct discrimination against an individual because someone **thinks** they may have a protected characteristic.

An example could include someone assuming Leila is gay and discriminating against her because she wears an AIDS ribbon. The individual being discriminated against does not actually have to possess the characteristic which the discriminator thinks they possess.

Making adjustments for a disabled colleague

Where a colleague (including a potential colleague) has a disability, City has a duty to make 'reasonable adjustments' to reduce any disadvantage that the colleague could be facing.

Example 1: a colleague could be allowed to work slightly different hours than the rest of the workforce, avoiding rush hour travel if they had a disability.

Example 2: a company policy is only to offer car parking spaces to senior managers. However, a colleague who is not a manager has developed a mobility impairment and needs to park very close to the building. If the colleague is allocated a parking space this is likely to be a reasonable adjustment to the car parking policy.

Example 3: Clear glass doors at the end of a corridor present a hazard for a visually impaired colleague. Brightly coloured strips at eye level that can be seen more easily by the colleague would be classed as a reasonable adjustment to the workplace

Example 4: As a reasonable adjustment the employer provides specialist software for a colleague who has developed a visual impairment. Their job involves using a computer and software enables them to continue in their role.

Indirect Discrimination
Indirect discrimination can occur when a condition, rule, policy or practice in a company applies to everyone but particularly disadvantages people who share a protected characteristic.

It may be justified if the employer can show that they acted reasonably in managing the business (e.g. that it is a 'proportionate means of achieving a legitimate aim'.

Harassment & Victimisation
Introduction

Other forms of discrimination that can occur in the workplace are harassment and victimisation.

Harassment

Harassment is "unwanted conduct related to a relevant protected characteristic, which has the purpose or effect of violating an individual's dignity or creating an intimidating, hostile, degrading, humiliating or offensive environment for that individual".

It occurs because the victim possesses a "protected characteristic"

Harassment can consist of verbal abuse, racist jokes, insensitive comments, leering, physical contact, unwanted sexual advances, ridicule or isolation.

We have a duty of care to our colleagues to ensure they do not suffer from harassment within the workplace.

Perception of harassment

In each case, it is the victim's perception of this behaviour that makes it harassment, not the intentions of the harasser (who will often claim that it was "only a bit of fun")

So, an example would be, if Mylene's male colleagues addressed her as 'gorgeous', she could legitimately complain and expect not only an apology but that the name calling stopped.

In addition, others who are not directly subjected to the harassment can complain if they find such behaviour offensive.

Victimisation

Victimisation occurs when an individual is treated less favourably than others because they made, tried to make or supported a complaint of discrimination under the Equality Act.

In order to be protected under the Act, the original complaint must have been made in good faith.

Someone making a malicious complaint or supporting an untrue one is not protected.

Test your knowledge so far...

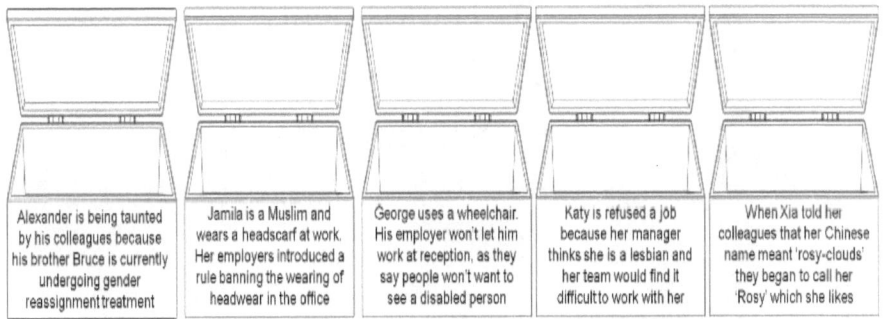

| Alexander is being taunted by his colleagues because his brother Bruce is currently undergoing gender reassignment treatment | Jamila is a Muslim and wears a headscarf at work. Her employers introduced a rule banning the wearing of headwear in the office | George uses a wheelchair. His employer won't let him work at reception, as they say people won't want to see a disabled person | Katy is refused a job because her manager thinks she is a lesbian and her team would find it difficult to work with her | When Xia told her colleagues that her Chinese name meant 'rosy-clouds' they began to call her 'Rosy' which she likes |

Test your knowledge (cont'd)

You provide a witness statement in support of a colleague who's raised a grievance about homophobic bullying at work. Your employer thinks both you and your colleague are being over sensitive and reject the grievance and a subsequent appeal.

A few months later you apply for a promotion but your application is turned down although you're able to show you have the necessary skills and experience. Your manager says you're a trouble-maker as you helped your colleague and therefore you shouldn't be promoted.

This is an example of
1. Harassment
2. Victimization
3. Discrimination

CHAPTER THREE

Key Equality Issues

Introduction

Equality at work should apply to all colleagues throughout their working life: from recruitment & selection right through to retirement.

The tabs below provide some information on the steps that City currently takes to ensure that we as a business comply with the Equality Act together with some good practice advice that will help you with some of the key equality issues faced in the workplace.

Recruitment & Induction

The wording in a job description should be clear and straightforward and the **use of language** should be clear. For example, instead of saying "needs to be physically fit" it should be more specific and say "needs to reach and bend to pick items from shelves". Terms like 'mature person' or 'young graduate' may be considered discriminatory.

It is unlawful to ask health related questions **before** making a job offer except in order to determine if a candidate can carry out a function which is **essential** to the job. At interview **do not** ask questions of a discriminatory nature (e.g. about marital status or asking a female if she plans to have children)

Be mindful of any notes taken during a job interview and make sure they are not discriminatory. Both colleagues and potential candidates have the right to see any information held about them.

Training & Development

All colleagues should have the same access to training, whether they are part-time or full-time.

Flexibility is important when it comes to training workshops - e.g. residential training may not suit those with caring responsibilities or those who work from home

Don't make assumptions about who will want training or the benefits is may bring, for example:

- woman won't be interested because they have children; if a worker is older they will not want to continue to learn and develop; or a younger worker will quickly move on so investment in their development is a waste of time.
- a disabled person's ability to take part in training or to the benefits it will bring. Be prepared to talk to your disabled colleague and find out whether they need reasonable adjustments to participate fully.

Promotion

We must offer opportunities for promotion, transfer or other career development without unlawful discrimination. This includes opportunities that could lead to permanent promotion (e.g. stepping up on a temporary promotion, deputising or secondment)

Imagine an employer who only allows colleagues who work full-time to apply for promotion. This could have a significant impact on women workers, who are more likely to work part-time. Unless an employer can objectively justify the requirement to work full-time, this is very likely to be indirect discrimination because of sex.

Equal Pay

-
-

The Equality Act 2010 covers the right of women to equal pay with men for equal work, both for part-time and full-time colleagues.

Additionally, as a business we need to ensure that people who share a protected characteristic are not disadvantaged compared to people who do not share it.

An equal pay audit helps to make sure that the business is making the right decision when it comes to pay and benefits and is good practice for avoiding unlawful discrimination in pay and benefits.

Getting it Wrong

Sometimes people (companies and individuals) don't always abide by the rules - either to the minimum standards set out by the law or to those they have set themselves.

Let's take a look at the different costs incurred in some real-life situations.

Click on each of the tabs on the left to learn more about the potential costs of getting it wrong.

Type 'workplace discrimination claim' into Google and you're almost guaranteed to read about a new case hitting the headlines every single week.

The financial costs to an employer, if a case is won, can be enormous.

Lets take a look at a couple of different cases that have made the news.

Click here to watch a short video about Dr Eval Michalak, a consultant physician, who was awarded £4.5million compensation for workplace discrimination trauma

Click here to read about Nigel McArthur, a former pre-constructional manager, who was awarded a six figure sum after being 'bullied' out of his job.

What is a reputation worth? In today's highly competitive world, companies that lose credibility because of a failure to be consistent about equality are at risk of suffering from serious reputational damage.

Imagine just for a minute that you see a job advertisement for a company that has made the headlines for disability, sexual or racial discrimination. *(or any other type of discrimination)*

Would you want to work for that company? I'm sure I wouldn't!

Furthermore, if you were a customer, would you want to give that company your business or trust your business in their hands?

A company's reputation is one of its biggest and most important assets. When people hear and say great things about a company and its good standing is reported in the media it may receive even more customer enquiries, retain the very best colleagues, see increased profits and be able to grow it operations.

After a public relations disaster, the reputation a company has worked hard to build can easily be destroyed - and may be nearly impossible to rebuild.

It has been said that job satisfaction is lowest when a person is discriminated against in the workplace. They will feel deflated, stop caring about the business and develop negative feelings. There is a direct link between loyalty, retention and discrimination. People are more likely to be looking for other jobs when they feel they have been ill-treated.

They'll jump at the first opportunity they get.

Turnover costs can be huge. Between advertising a position, reviewing and pre-screening prospective applicants, interviewing, making final decisions, inducting and training, hiring a new colleague can cost thousands of pounds.

Other costs can include:

•   overtime payments

- missed deadlines
- interruptions to the flow of work
- higher levels of stress related absence
- long term workers becoming unsettled and leaving.

CHAPTER FOUR

Diverse People, Diverse Identities

When we talk about diversity, we don't just talk about race and ethnicity.

Diversity includes **all different people**, each contributing their own uniqueness, making the UK a more interesting place to live.

So diversity includes people of different **gender, ages, sexual orientation, disability, religion, beliefs** and more.

It is important that everyone respects and celebrates each other's differences' so we can all get along, learn from each other and share an exciting mix of cultures and experiences

Our commitment to managing diversity

We are committed to encouraging diversity amongst all of our colleagues and our aim is that our colleagues will be truly representative of all areas of society and that each colleague feels respected and able to work to their full potential.

Sub-consciously you will look for evidence to support your original assumption. In other words, we see what we want to see and hear what we want to hear, filtering out anything that is contrary to our assumption.

Assumptions can lead to misunderstandings and a lack of communication, because you think you already **KNOW** the answer or understand what is going on. You can also take things personally and feel awkward about a situation so you ignore it, or gossip about it to others while avoiding contact with the person concerned.

Many of our assumptions remain untested, yet we *believe* them to be true and use them as a benchmark to discount people.

This limits their future potential and any possibilities because you've already labelled them.

In other words, it's easy to write someone off, not include them in something, and ignore their potential for learning and growth.

Believing your assumptions means that you will underestimate or disregard people, often without even having a conversation with them.

Your imagination makes things up when you don't understand something and an assumption is created about its meaning.

Finally, when the truth is revealed, you may find you've totally misunderstood the whole situation and gotten it horribly wrong. Here are some of the potential outcomes of making assumptions. You will:

- Lose trust in others.
- Become more reactive.
- Stop the growth and development of others.
- Miss opportunities.
- Limit the potential of the team.
- Risk direct / indirect discrimination

We tend to look for mirror images of ourselves in others. We assume that others think and feel the same way as we do and make the same judgments. We imagine the truth and don't see the reality of how things are or the potential for what could be.

Recognise when you are making assumptions – this sounds simple but it takes a lot of practice.

Challenge / Test your assumptions - How do you know that what you are thinking is real? What evidence do you have? You might be wrong! Check in on your own thinking and turn it around. Once you begin questioning your assumptions regularly you'll find doing so becomes easy. You'll learn and grow as a result and are likely to improve your understanding of other people.

Look for the potential in others – Don't write people off too quickly with sweeping statements. People's potential is unlimited. They may not be good at something today, but if you give them the tools, opportunity, support and encouragement to learn, you could help them transform their potential and performance.

Invest time with people - our colleagues and our customers.

Zero Tolerance

Behaviour that is considered bullying by one person may be acceptable by another.

Most people will agree on extreme cases of bullying and harassment, however it is the varying perception of behaviours that cause most problems.

City's Equality Policy gives you more information on the definitons of bullying and harassment but the types of behaviour that will not be tolerated are:

- Malicious rumour spreading
- Sending email gossip (e.g. information that people do not need to know about in order to be able to do their job)
- Ridiculing someone or demeaning them, or setting them up to fail

- Unwelcome advances (e.g. touching, standing too close, display of offensive materials, asking for sexual favours, making decisions on the basis of sexual advances being accepted or rejected
- Making threats or comments about job security without foundation
- Deliberately undermining or constantly criticising a colleague
- Preventing a colleague's progression by intentionally blocking promotion or training opportunities

Modern Slavery
What is Modern Slavery?
Slavery has a devastating impact on individual victims. It also affects businesses from a reputational, legal financial and operational perspective. Click on the image to learn more.
Types of slavery
Modern Slavery captures a whole range of types of exploitation. Click on the image to learn more
Why do I need to know?
Freeing the nation from these cruel acts is a responsibility for us all. Click on the image to read more.

Recognising the signs

Some of the signs are often hidden. Click on the image to read more about the indicators of Modern Slavery.

CHAPTER FIVE

Modern Slavery - The context

In 2013, the National Referral Mechanism, the UK's victim identification and support process, received 1746 referrals of potential victims - almost a 50 percent increase on 2012 figures.

The 1746 referrals comprised 1,122 female (64%) and 624 male (36%) [potential] victims. 1295 (74%) were adults and 451 (26%) were children.

But these are just the victims that are known about. Modern Slavery is a largely covert crime: victims tend to be controlled and hidden away.

Question 1 of 10

Natalie's former manager is approached by a prospective employer asking for a reference because she has applied for a job with them. The manager says he cannot recommend Natalie, as her decision to 'come out' as bisexual was disruptive, and lists a number of examples where he believed this resulted in team arguments, customer complaints and other colleagues quitting.

Which type of discrimination could this be?

Question 2 of 10

Nnamdi has a severe stammer and is claiming harassment against his line manager after she frequently teased and humiliated him about his disability. Richard, who shares an office with Nnamdi, is offended by the remarks and says it is creating an offensive environment for him too. What could Richard do in this case?

Question 3 of 10

June, a project manager, has been promised promotion by her manager. However, after she tells him that her mother, who lives at home, has cancer. He withdraws the promotion because he feels the commitment of looking after her mother and moving to a higher grade role will be too much for her.

What type of discrimination might this be?

Question 4 of 10

Abu is in his twenties. He is fully qualified and doing well in his current role. He's very ambitious and sees a role advertised that he thinks would help him take the next logical step in his career.

However, the advertisement specifies that candidates must have ten years' experience in the profession. Abu has six.

If Abu's application is not considered for this reason what type of discrimination might this be?

Question 5 of 10

You have a CV from a candidate whom you telephone interview and want to put forward for a role. They are called for interview. When you ring the candidate to confirm the interview date and time, at the end of the conversation , the candidate mentions that they are registered disabled – what is your response?

Question 6 of 10

Paul, a senior manager, turns down Angela's application for promotion to supervisor. Angela, a lesbian, learns that Paul did this because he believes the team she applied to manage are homophobic. He thought that her sexual orientation would prevent her from gaining the team's respect and managing them effectively.

What type of discrimination has Paul displayed?

Question 7 of 10

Dimitri is 45, but looks much younger. Many people assume he is in his mid-twenties. He is not allowed to represent the company at the annual meeting because the managing director thinks he is too young.

What type of discrimination could this be?

Question 8 of 10

Amelia tells Bryan, another colleague, that she has diabetes and needs to carry biscuits to eat when her blood sugar levels fall. Her manager has no knowledge about her disability and refuses to allow her, or any other colleagues, eat food at their desk. Amelia suffers a hypoglycemic attack.

What type of discrimination could Amelia successfully claim in this instance?

Question 9 of 10

What should you do in the first instance if you suspect that a colleague may be a victim of Modern Slavery?

Question 10 of 10

Halina makes a formal complaint against her manager because she feels she has been discriminated against because she is married. Although the complaint is resolved through the grievance procedure, Halina is subsequently ignored and excluded from work-related social events by her colleagues after they realised she had named them in a complaint.

What could Halina claim in this instance?